MW00938722

Searching

For More

Bobby Benavides

© Copyright 2017. All Rights Reserved.

Table of Contents

———

Where Are you Headed?

K ey Verse: "Your word is a lamp to my feet and a light to my path." Psalm 119:105 (NASB)

I constantly thank God for giving someone the mind to invent the GPS. I am horrible at reading maps, and I can only assume I would be pulling off the road trying to figure out the symbols regularly if I had to depend on paper maps to get around. I do not even want to imagine what my drive would be like without the devices we have now, but I am sure it would involve several U-turns.

You might relate to what I just confessed. You need a GPS because maps are like ancient Egyptian hieroglyphics. You need something that is telling you where to go or you will end up in another place very easily. Without a guide, you will be lost, and most likely, won't make it to your destination on time or even at all.

This is the same with your journey with Christ. The scriptures are meant to guide you in life. They are meant to give you direction. They are meant to lead you for a specific purpose. As you study scriptures and try to figure out how to apply it to your life, your journey shifts. You are no longer traveling on your own trying to figure out which way to turn, but you now have the Word of God leading your steps.

In order for a GPS or a map to really work, you need to know where you're headed, but you also have to listen and pay close attention to the things around you. I have had times where I was talking or listening to music and missed the turn. Then, I heard the voice yelling at me, "Make a U-Turn...NOW!" I might have added the "Now" part, but it might as well said that. Siri can be vicious!

Scripture tells you where to go and where you are going for the glory of God. Focus on the Word. Focus on the truth. Allow yourself to clear your mind and truly embrace the message Christ has for you in your journey.

In Psalm 119:105, the psalmist is writing to declare God's guidance in his life. He recognized God as being the clear leader in his journey and he had to follow the word of God to make the right steps on the way. God is directing the steps and He needs us to follow His ways.

When you know where you're headed with Christ as the lead, your trajectory is clear. Don't allow yourself to get distracted from the path He has you on. Listen to His voice and pay attention to the leading of the Spirit as you move forward.

The great thing about the Spirit is that most of the time, you won't feel dumb for missing the turn. He has a place for you; He just needs you headed that way.

QUESTION: How do you hear God's voice leading you in your life? What are some steps you can take to listen more to His direction?

NOTES

Finding Joy On The Journey

Key Verses: "You also became imitators of us and of the Lord, having received the word in much tribulation with the joy of the Holy Spirit, so that you became an example to all the believers..." 1 Thessalonians 1:6-7 (NASB)

Winnie The Pooh was one of my favorite cartoons growing up. I couldn't wait to introduce the characters to my children. I always felt like I could relate to Tigger with his bouncy nature, and his exuberance is something I resonated with.

However, Eeyore was the one character that I struggled to connect with. He was always gloomy. He couldn't see beyond the dark clouds. He struggled to find joy in anything. His life was dark, even with so much light around him.

As a kid, it was difficult to understand Eeyore, but as an adult, I have found myself grasping his character more. Life is hard. I know when I face any form of trial, it takes a lot out of me to focus on the joy of the Lord.

You might be the same way too. When you face hardship of any kind, you might feel defeated. The darkness might be so overwhelming that it is next to impossible to catch a glimpse of light around you. It is so easy to be an Eeyore.

The problem isn't the uncontrollable trial because that will not change, but the problem is your perspective on the trial. When faced with a difficulty in life, you must choose how you view your circumstances. You can be consumed by the gloom or you can search for the things that bring joy on your journey.

When you put your head down for too long in sorrow, you will miss the smiles around you. When you focus on your feet, you will miss the rainbow. God is constantly trying to reveal His promises of love and rest, but when we focus on ourselves, we will miss His message.

Paul shared in the key scripture passage that the joy of the Holy Spirit the Church received in their trial was an example for other believers. When other people see us handling our trial with joy, they will be encouraged to do the same. This does not mean walking around with a smile on our face all the time, but being honest about the challenge we are facing and walking with peace in our knowledge that God is in control and the Spirit is present.

The joy of the Lord is all around you. You need to lift up your head and find it along the way. Times will be hard, but you have a God who is good all the time. Find His joy for you today.

QUESTION: Where do you look for joy in times of struggle? What can you be doing to be a better example to those around you who need encouragement in their trials?

NOTES

DAY 3

Who Is With You?

K ey Verses: "...and let us consider how to stimulate one another to love and good deeds, not forsaking our own assembling together, as is the habit of some, but encouraging one another; and all the more as you see the day drawing near." Hebrews 10:24-25 (NASB)

I have always enjoyed sports. I like watching sports on television, but I also enjoy going to live events in stadiums. Being around other people cheering for their respective team is a wonderful experience. The energy and excitement around you when something thrilling occurs is beyond explanation.

Although I find sports to be exhilarating, I have come to realize that I don't really enjoy watching them alone. If I am home alone watching a game, I feel like I am unengaged and not as interested compared to when others are around me. I have never attended a live sporting event by myself and I doubt I ever would.

I feel like this is a sign of our internal need for a community. We need to have people with us. I have never met anyone who enjoys taking long drives alone. I have never met anyone who enjoys site seeing by themselves, but if they do, they will take plenty of pictures to share on social media in order for their internet community to connect with their journey.

You see, God has wired all of us for community. He has made you and me to be together. Your life experience is not meant to be lived alone. You need people with you as you walk and maneuver through your journey.

The author of Hebrews supports the idea that you need a community in the key passage. It shows that you cannot be left alone in your faith or you might fade. The encouragement you receive with other believers is how you will continue to walk in a healthy relationship with Jesus and others. You need to have a group of people you are being empowered, authentic and edified with. It is healthy for them and you.

Living in this world can be quite lonely without a connection. Find a good group of people or an individual you can relate with, so you may grow together in unity. God wants you to search for more, but He wants you to be linked with other members of creation in the process of discovering who you are in Him.

QUESTION: Who do you have walking with you in life? What can you do to increase your engagement in an authentic community?

NOTES

Running On E

K ey Verse: And He has said to me, "My grace is sufficient for you, for power is perfected in weakness." Most gladly, therefore, I will rather boast about my weaknesses, so that the power of Christ may dwell in me. 2 Corinthians 12:9 (NASB)

Have you ever let your fuel tank get so low that the warning light turns on? It's amazing how one light can cause your heart to race and your sweat pour out, especially if you can't find a sign telling you when the next gas station is coming up. When that light pops on and you hear the ding, you know you're in trouble.

The reality is, you have the same light inside of you. You know when you have worn yourself out. You know when your fuel level is low and you are experiencing burnout. Your body gives you warning signs that it is about to shut down, and many times, you will do whatever it takes to make sure you don't run on empty.

You know you need to refill your system, so you will take a vacation or sick days. You will find a way to retreat and relax. You will get the medicine you need to heal and replenish what you have been lacking. The fact is, you won't let your body give out, so you'll take care of it and come back stronger.

What about your spiritual life?

The Holy Spirit informs us of our emptiness. There may not be a light that flashes or a sound to signal your impending doom, but if your spiritual connection with God is flailing, you will sense it. It will manifest itself in different ways. You might find yourself easily angered. You might find yourself unable to experience joy in your life. You might find it more difficult to love people. The list could go on and on.

When you find yourself at this place of spiritual emptiness in your journey, you should be more apt to find healing as you are when you're physically empty. Find a place of refuge in Jesus. Find comfort with other friends who are believers and allow them to pray with and for you. Replenish your soul in retreat to meditate on God's word and listen for His voice in your life.

If your spiritual fuel light is blinking because you're running on empty, search for God to refuel. He is easier to find than a gas station.

QUESTION: Where do you go when you're feeling spiritually empty?

NOTES

_____

_____

_____

_____

_____

_____

_____

_____

_____

_____

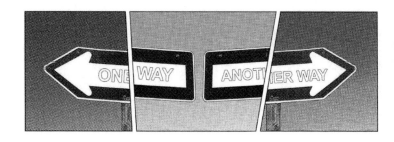

Watch For The Signs

K ey Verse: "But if any of you lacks wisdom, let him ask of God, who gives to all generously and without reproach, and it will be given to him." James 1:5 (NASB)

If you're anything like me, you must have been at a place in life where you were longing for a sign. You sit and wait, but there is nothing happening that gives you clarity. You are longing for an answer and you grow impatient. You begin to question, "Am I doing this right? Am I praying enough? Am I looking in the right place?" It can be stressful.

You can grow frustrated when you don't have your decisions spelled out for you. The problem is, you might be looking for specific signs and God is trying to reveal His guidance in other ways. He doesn't come with a loud gong, but a soft whisper.

Often times, the signs you expect to find are within you. God has given a clear leading in how you should live your life, but He hasn't given such clarity in the way you should go. However, He has given you desires and passions. He has shown you where your heart gets excited. He has shown you where your mind is exhilarated and inspired.

You may not know what direction you're supposed to go, but you do know what moves you. As you pursue your goal, figure out where your passion is being drawn and move towards that. God will guide you as you move forward.

James reminds us that our wisdom comes from God. We need to seek Him fully so we may know the direction He wants us to go. The signs are available to us, but understanding the signs only comes through seeking the wisdom necessary to figure out what is being shown.

The hardest part of following God's lead is trusting He knows where you're going better than you do. We have to walk in faith, knowing that He is the one who put the signs in place and He won't lead you astray.

QUESTION: Why do you find it difficult to trust God with every aspect of your life? Write down your thoughts and lift them up to God. Allow Him to take the lead.

NOTES

Follow The Path

K ey Verse: "for we walk by faith, not by sight"
2 Corinthians 5:7 (NASB)

"I am at a fork in the road" is a common expression when people are making decisions. They see hope in both directions, but each of the roads come with their own sets of obstacles.

One way has more clarity than the other, but it might be so secure that your faith isn't being challenged, so you are hesitant. Yet, the other path is not so clear, but you know that it will stretch you and cause you to depend on God more, so you would be walking with timidity into the unknown.

What are you supposed to do?

When I was in college, I had a professor tell me, "Bobby, 'whenever one door closes, another one opens' is a false concept we have fallen for. When God is in the lead, one door might close, but several open. If you are seeking God with all you have and trust His guidance, then wherever you step, He will be there with you."

I have held onto those words ever since I heard them.

When you are faced with a fork in the road, step back and seek God. Seek assistance from those close to you who share the same faith as you to have them join you in prayer. Allow yourself time to think about where you are headed. Then, step onto the path and go.

The reality is, God is in control. He knows where He wants you to go. If you believe in the sovereignty of God, then where you step, is where He wanted you anyway.

Your faith in God can be confirmed and strengthened by your willingness to step forward. It is not about what you see, that would be too easy, but it is about what you don't see. If you knew what was coming your way, you would coast through life without the need of perseverance.

It might not be an easy path, but we must follow the path He is leading us on. Trust His presence. Allow your faith to grow and walk with Him whichever direction you choose.

No matter what, He is present, and He is in the lead.

QUESTION: Do you have people you can call on to pray with you during hard decisions? If not, find one or two. If you do, let them know and pray with them regularly.

NOTES

Flat Tires

K ey Verse: Every good thing given and every perfect gift is from above, coming down from the Father of lights, with whom there is no variation or shifting shadow. James 1:17 (NASB)

I used to love riding my bike when I was a kid. I would ride it to the store, to my friend's house, to school, and to my grandma's house. I loved my bike.

The bike was a black Schwinn Beach Cruiser with white wall tires. The handle bars had black foam covering and the spokes were clean. The seat was black leather and I would clean it with leather protector regularly to keep it shiny. I learned quickly I had to let it dry before I sat on it, but I tried my best to keep the bike in great shape.

One day, I was getting ready to jump on my bike and go over to my friend's house. I looked at the bike and something was wrong. The seat was shiny, the tires were clean, the spokes sparkled in the sunlight, but the clean tires were flat. Both of them.

I was devastated.

I went to the bike shop and found out that they had to special-order my tubes, but it was only going to take a couple of days. Again, another setback. I wanted to ride my bike, but I had to wait until the necessary supplies arrived.

In your faith journey, you will experience flat tires. There will be setbacks. You will expect everything to be perfect, but then you will receive news that shifts everything. The air is seriously let out of your tires.

You can both get depressed and feel like everything is ruined or you can respond by seeking assistance. God is like the bike shop. The bike shop had to order the parts and they were the only people who could get what I needed. God is the same way.

God might not get you what you want right away, but He will respond in due time with what you need.

In my time without the bike, I gained an enjoyment for walking. I was able to look around more. I was able to notice a house with live peacocks in their yard that I had never noticed while riding my bike.

When I got my bike running again, I was happy, but I definitely loved the experiences I gained while walking. God might need us to change our perspective on life, so flat tires have to happen.

Allow God to teach you in your flat tire experiences. Allow God to reveal things that you might be missing in life as you wait for the tires to be repaired.

Enjoy the ride.

QUESTION: When your plans get hindered or halted, do you find yourself seeking God's wisdom or dwelling in your trial? When faced with a "flat tire," write down your response to God and listen for His guidance.

NOTES

Hazards Ahead

K ey Verse: "In this you greatly rejoice, even though now for a little while, if necessary, you have been distressed by various trials."
1 Peter 1:6

At one time, I was employed by one of the largest non-profit Christian humanitarian organizations in the world. I was serving youth and families in rural West Virginia. I loved my job. I had great benefits, great co-workers, and I felt secure.

In fact, I felt so secure that I had told my wife to resign from her job to pursue her career goals. Then, three months after my wife resigned, I received notice that my position would be eliminated due to budget cuts. To add more stress, we just had our first child a few months before we received this news.

I was stressed and concerned. I had no idea what was going to happen. The organization took good care of me in the months leading up to my last day, but I was still nervous about what would be coming our way.

I went through several different emotions as the end of my time drew near. I was confused. I mean, everything was going so well, how could this happen? I was sad. I loved my role, and I could see myself there for a long time. I was serving God too, so why would things not work out?

God had bigger plans in my struggles. I just had to remain focused on Him.

I have come to the conclusion that these are the hazard signs you are warned against while traveling.

The fallen rocks. The deer that might be crossing. The warning of the possible icy bridge ahead. The road is supposed to be clear for the trip, but there is always a possibility of a delay or a complete change in your mapped out travel.

Many of you might find yourself in a similar situation. A life-changing detour on your life journey occurs. Everything could be going very well in your life and you could be feeling good about not witnessing any fallen rocks, but suddenly, you will find a boulder in the middle of both lanes.

So, what do you do?

All too often when people come to follow Jesus, they expect things to be easy from that point on. However, Christ never promised that. You will face trials of many kinds, but if Christ is your center, then you will handle the hazards. You will know how to maneuver through the obstacles.

Your trip is important, but you need to remain patient and focused on the road. Do not allow the hazards to hinder your focus.

You might lose a job that was supposed to last forever. You may have a relationship end after many years of being together. You may see your financial situation struggle when you were feeling secure for retirement.

There are many other issues that could cause you to stress, but when you are resting in the word of God and trusting in Christ, your vision should be clear and you should find comfort in the truth of scripture.

Focus on Christ, not the roadblocks.

QUESTION: Why do you allow "hazards" to distract you from your destination?

NOTES

Watch The Stop Lights

K EY VERSES: "We know that the law is spiritual; but I am unspiritual, sold as a slave to sin. I do not understand what I do. For what I want to do I do not do, but what I hate I do. And if I do what I do not want to do, I agree that the law is good." Romans 7:14-16 (NASB)

Thanks to a dear lady from church; my family and I ate at Applebee's one night, and we had a delicious meal! I'm not sure if it was because it was a late meal, so anything would taste good, or it was really that good?!

Although the food was good, that wasn't the highlight of the meal. Applebee's has done a total overhaul of their brand in the past couple years and their bags have some new artwork on them.

On the bottom of their bag, there was a phrase that caught my eye:

"Cravings Don't Like Stoplights"

I instantly thought of my life as a follower of Christ and went straight to the sacrifices I need to make to maintain a healthy relationship with my Savior.

Then, there's us collectively as the body of Christ and our call to live in such a way that we honor God in all that we do.

Our sinful nature tries to call us to move against our God. Our sinful nature beckons us to push our Savior aside in order to satisfy our "cravings" and appease our appetites for destructive behaviors or actions.

Our selfish desire will cause a battle within, which is against the Spirit. The Spirit speaks clearly to us, although quietly, He speaks to us guiding our steps. The quiet voice is sharing wisdom and our selfishness is screaming foolishness!

When we are about to move towards an action that will pull us down and distract us from the wisdom of Scripture, we need to listen to the warnings that flash within. The war will ensue. The struggle will become more apparent because we will be fighting against what we want to do when we know what we should do.

The stoplights that Jesus throws up for us cause our sinful cravings to get in an uproar. In fact, they tend to become stronger than ever. Our sinful nature wants to prove that we are still independent and we can do whatever we want. Our sinful nature is moving us away from where we need to be.

FOCUS!

The stoplights are ahead; slow down. Focus on the truth of Christ. Focus on what He has done to redeem us from the sin we face. We need to recognize our humanity and our limitations. We need to listen for the guidance of the Spirit and move towards Him.

Sin will always come calling and our appetite will try to get the best of us, but we need to rest in God's will power. He is the One that will give us the strength to stand against the struggle. He is the One that will win the war.

We cannot do this on our own.

Our cravings will hate us for stopping, but in the end, our appetite will go towards what we know is righteous.

When we seek to live a faithful life, our humanity will resist what is good, but if we are a new creation in Christ, then our soul will thirst for righteousness!

May we calm the grumbling of sinful cravings by resting in the stillness of God's righteousness.

May we strive to live a life of healthy connection with Christ and make a great effort to withstand our desires indulge in depravity.

Our cravings hate stoplights, but our God loves it when we wait to hear His voice before we go.

Peace and blessings, friends.

QUESTION: Do you turn to Scripture or prayer when you feel the desire to sin?

NOTES

The Fog Will Fade

K ey Verse: "Then Jesus again spoke to them, saying, 'I am the Light of the world; he who follows Me will not walk in the darkness, but will have the Light of life.'" John 8:12 (NASB)

Have you ever had to drive through a fog? Fog makes things difficult on the road, especially when I have to drive through construction zones. I have to keep my headlights on and my eyes open for deer, other cars, or even people and hope I don't make any drastic mistakes.

Fog hits at the most inopportune times. Sometimes, I have to wait for awhile until the fog clears enough to start driving. Often times, when caught in a fog, confusion can set in.

Sometimes in life, we hit a fog. It's a rough point that causes distraction and frustration. It comes in so many different forms. We face the fog that causes us to stay put and not move forward. We may have an experience that is light enough to move through, but we still stride cautiously, waiting for the unforeseen obstacles to come. No matter what kind of fog we experience, it is still a hindrance.

However, one of the things I have come to recognize about fog is, sooner or later, the light burns it off. As the day progresses, the fog dissipates. We can see clearly and we know where we are headed.

When we face the fog in life, remember there is a God who is the light of the world. He will help you get through and sooner or later, your fog will dissipate and you will know where you're going.

I have gained some insight that might prove useful as you travel through the fog and you start to see the light: put your sunglasses on and enjoy the rest of your ride because the destination is coming up.

Question: When does your fog set in? Do you have a place or person to go to when you are in the place of confusion?

NOTES

Making The Right Moves

K ey Verses: "Two are better than one, because they have a good return for their labor: If either of them falls down, one can help the other up. But pity anyone who falls and has no one to help them up." Ecclesiastes 4:9-10 (NASB)

The other day I was driving behind an SUV shedding ice chips. Ok, really, it was as if the SUV had just hit an iceberg and it had pieces flying off. I was having a blast discovering what kind of handling my vehicle had during a snowy evening.

Anyway, as I was switching lanes, slowing down, braking, dodging, and any other maneuver I could legally do, I started thinking. Dodging the shrapnel was intense and made me think I was a great stunt driver.

Sometimes, we run into people like this SUV, especially people who are trying to figure out their relationship with Jesus. There are shells covering the pain or past that an individual has experienced. When they come to a breaking point, pieces start to fly.

Often times, we find ourselves in the path of the pieces. Their shell starts to break and we have to maneuver through the flying shrapnel. It is difficult.

When this occurs, we make several decisions behind the "SUV." We can change directions if we can find an exit that we can take quickly; we might brake abruptly and keep our distance in order to avoid being hit, or we stay close and just hope that the pieces don't do too much damage.

We have to be smart in our decision making. Some people need us to be willing to risk our distance and remain close. Others call for us to brake and step back and allow the pieces to come off before we get closer. Finally, we need to be wise enough to know when we need to leave them completely and find a safer route.

It is hard to discern when we should take one of these steps, but it is essential to search. Pain is part of life. People willing to work through it will have the shrapnel, but it won't be too hard to work through. The person who is trying to work through it, but keeps drawing you in to the hurt instead of working through the hurt with you, may require you to brake off and keep some distance. Finally, the person who piles their pain on you and doesn't want to get help or work it out, but expects you to keep helping or being piled on, is screaming for you to take an exit.

Be aware of your situation. Be aware of the individuals in your life that are draining you, but also those who need you to be patient.

Ultimately, while you're driving in life, you need to be safe and gingerly maneuver through the hurt of others and be ready to make the necessary steps to keep moving forward.

QUESTION: How have you handled taking on too much "shrapnel" from another person?

NOTES

_____

_____

_____

_____

_____

_____

_____

_____

_____

_____

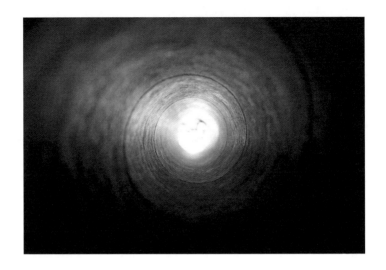

Tunnel Vision

K EY VERSES: "Then Jesus said to His disciples, "If anyone wishes to come after Me, he must deny himself, and take up his cross and follow Me. For whoever wishes to save his life will lose it; but whoever loses his life for My sake will find it." Matthew 16:24-25

I remember when I took driver's education class in high school. They would talk about all the issues a driver might experience on the road and the teacher took the opportunity to strike fear in every student in the class.

In one of his lectures, he went into detail about Tunnel Vision. He wanted all of the students to be aware of this possibility. Out of all the lectures the teacher gave, this one stuck with me the most.

I don't know why, but for some reason, I was truly terrified of being so focused on what was in front of me, that I would miss what was around me. I played out every possible scenario from merging off a cliff to cutting off a minivan with a soccer team as passengers.

I am full of irrational fears.

However, when I consider my faith journey, I believe I have been guilty of tunnel vision and many other people who claim Jesus struggle with it today.

Far too often, I have found myself focused on my own life. I have discovered that I can be quite self-centered and ignore some of the needs around me. As I focus so much on myself, I fail to recognize the struggles of others, and it hinders me from being a representation of Christ in the lives of the most hurting.

It is not that my issues are not important and shouldn't be dealt with, but I need to find balance. My pain needs to be acknowledged, but it cannot overtake my ability to empathize with others in their trials.

Can you relate?

Have you ever found yourself so wrapped up in your own life that you miss opportunities to care for those who are going through hard times? Have you ever been so focused on getting your own success that you failed to lift someone up to succeed? Have you ever felt like your life issues were more important than others?

The tunnel vision we experience causes us to miss the chance to be the Church for others. Having tunnel vision limits our ability to show we care and give compassionate service and can hinder the spiritual journey of another.

I have realized that there are so many people hurting in this world and I miss opportunities to serve because I am in a hurry to meet my own needs.

We all have to slow ourselves down. We need to open our eyes and check our surroundings. The tunnel vision of life is causing us to lose out on blessing others and serving for the glory of God.

Christ called His disciples to live sacrificially. He called them to deny their self and follow. When we follow Jesus completely, then His desires become our desires. Through the Scripture, we find that His desire is to love the least and the lost. To serve the poor and oppressed. He took the time to step into the lives of the hurting and bring healing and peace.

Our schedules and personal lives are important, but God's call is urgent. We can ignore the commission of Christ to teach what He taught and make disciples (Matthew 28), so we must be willing to sacrifice our time to influence the lives of the hurting.

May we come to see our time is most valuable when it is spent glorifying our Creator. May we come to realize the parts of our lives that tunnel vision has hindered us from serving. May we serve lovingly with compassion and empathy for the kingdom of God to be realized in the lives of the broken.

QUESTION: How has tunnel vision influenced your faith?

NOTES

Don't Be Afraid To Pump Your Brakes

K EY VERSE: "There is an appointed time for everything. And there is a time for every event under heaven" Ecclesiastes 3:1 (NASB)

Busyness seems to be celebrated lately. It is always interesting to me how people like to announce how overwhelmed they are with their schedule.

It's pretty sad.

I've been in meetings with people who constantly check their watch. I have been to youth sporting events and overheard parents talking about what they had to do after the game or the practice. It seems like a vicious cycle for many of them. They can't slow down.

I often wonder if people are afraid to slow down. I wonder if they are afraid of what they will discover about their own self if they hit the brakes. Perhaps they would have to own up to flaws or work on reconciling relationships if they truly decided to cut back their schedule.

When we pump our brakes we protect ourselves from burning out. We actually find ourselves creating healthy space to enjoy what is important.

Don't get so caught up in your schedule that you miss out on life. Don't get so overbooked that you don't have time to spend with your Creator. You need to slow down so you can observe where you are and where you are headed.

Don't be afraid to pump your brakes and seek God's message in your life. If you're going too fast, you might just miss His voice guiding you.

QUESTION: What would happen for you if you truly slowed down in your life?

NOTES

Tune-Up Needed

K EY VERSE: "For everyone who asks receives, and he who seeks finds, and to him who knocks it will be opened." Matthew 7:8

I remember when I received my first car. My grandma and grandpa came rolling into my driveway with a maroon 1965 El Camino. I was ecstatic!

I had just turned 18 and I wasn't sure what I would be driving to and from classes for college or work. My answer was found in that beautiful vehicle.

It had a gear shift on the column, also known as "Three-on-a-Tree," and I had to learn how to drive with a clutch. It was fantastic!

The original engine was a straight six. That was it. There were no computers and fancy gadgets, it was a simple motor that I could climb under the hood and work on. I seriously loved that car!

The only problem was, there were no lights letting me know something was wrong, I had to listen to the car. I had to know how the car ran when everything was fine. I had to pay attention to the misfires or slow start. I had to pay attention to my tires and make sure they were properly inflated with a tire gauge. It was my responsibility to recognize my vehicle's issues and respond appropriately.

I remember the first time my car backfired. It jerked and let out a loud bang that made people duck and cover when it went off. I was nervous.

The truth is, I didn't know what to do to fix it. I asked my dad and my grandfather what to do and they walked me through the process of fixing my spark plugs and checking the wires. It was fun, but I was concerned that I would mess it up pretty bad. My car needed a tune-up and I'm glad I had some people around who could guide me in the right direction.

For many of us, we need to receive "Tune-Ups" in our faith. Sometimes, we become stagnant in our journey and our spiritual growth begins to stall out.

Far too often, this happens with people who have been walking with Jesus for a while and begin to think they have heard it all. They begin to believe that there is nothing new to experience or learn and they stop reading or praying. They begin to stop going to church and being involved with a group of believers. Then, when things start getting tough, they realize that their spiritual engine isn't running the way it should.

The problem is, so many try to fix it on their own. They don't ask for wisdom or guidance from people who might have been there before. In fact, most people who have been walking with Christ for some time have most likely had a time where their faith journey struggled. So, it is a valuable practice to seek direction from an experienced follower of Jesus.

Could this be you?

Have you been feeling a spiritual misfire occurring in your soul? How have you responded?

Just like my car was backfiring and I needed to fix it right away before it got worse, you need to step into the garage and work under the hood.

Pray, ask, seek, and listen for God's direction. He is still there. He isn't the one with the struggling engine. In fact, He is the only one who can repair it.

It might be time to assess your faith engine and make sure you are firing on all cylinders, especially if you are searching for more in your relationship with Jesus.

QUESTION: What are some ways you can receive a tune-up in your faith?

NOTES

The Vanity Plate

K EY VERSE: Therefore, we are ambassadors for Christ, as though God were making an appeal through us; we beg you on behalf of Christ, be reconciled to God. 2 Corinthians 5:20

An interesting phenomenon that has been occurring on many vehicles is the "vanity plate." In 2016, Virginia offered the largest amount of vanity plate options. People were requesting different plates with identifiers.

It seems that many people want to be sure others know what they do or the nicknames they earned at some point in their life. I also believe they find joy in causing the driver behind them to be distracted while trying to figure out their puzzle.

The reality is, the vanity plate is fun. It is like a tattoo for your car. It is a way to make the car yours and give it a personality. Several people might have the same vehicle as you, but nobody has your "HOOPSTR" plate telling of your basketball prowess, and that is the important thing...right?

What if we looked at our lives as a gigantic Vanity Plate? What if we would think about what message we are sending on a daily basis?

What would your "Vanity Plate" look like to people around you? Would it be a clear message that brings people closer to Christ or is it vague and hard to understand that makes people wonder who or what you really represent?

When Paul shared that "...we are ambassadors for Christ," he was telling the readers that their lives spoke on behalf of Jesus. They had to constantly look at their reflection and make sure it was the image of Jesus and not their sinful self. They were guiding people to a reconciled relationship with their Creator, so their life had to reflect that call.

The words they used, the love they shared, the service they provided, and everything else they did was spreading the message of Christ to the world around them. The message they carried was a Vanity Plate for Christ and people knew what it said and who they represented.

The same call is passed on to all who claim the name of Jesus and walk as a follower of His teaching.

We always need to be wise about our words and actions. The people around us are trying to see if our lives match up with what we have on our plates.

Let your plate be clear and may people long to follow behind you because you live out what you claim to represent for the glory of Jesus.

QUESTION: What can you be doing differently today to make sure your plate is revealing a healthy message of Jesus?

NOTES

I hope you enjoyed the devotional.

If you would like to connect,
please feel free to contact me at:

bobby@bobbybenavides.me

instagram: @bobby_benavides

twitter: @bobben74

website: http://bobbybenavides.me